TWO THOUSAND RAINS

poems

KAREN MIREAU

Karen Mireau Books
Sonoma . California

ISBN: 978-1-943471-95-9

Cover Photo
by Karen Mireau

for all those
who know the grace & gravity
of loss

contents

preface

These poems are ones written over the course of my writing life from my early childhood to the present day, when I am now nearing the age of seventy.

I knew that I was being called to be a poet at the age of three. One winter of legendary cold, I stood on the banks of the St. Lawrence River near my grandmother's cottage on Point Vivian in Alexandria Bay, New York. The river was frozen solid and the black ice so thick a car could drive across it — or so I heard my parents say.

A storm was brewing. As the wind began to shift dramatically to the north and sterling clouds began to mass and darken and cantilever over the ice towards Canada, I was filled with astonishment — the kind that enters and completely captivates your soul-self. At that moment, I was awakened from my unversed child consciousness to a new and highly-heightened state of awareness. Every sight, every sound, every sensation became endowed with meaning.

My fate was certain to me on that day. Never once did I question or doubt that it would be my life task to say just what makes our connection to the natural world and to one another so profoundly sacred. Even though I did not have the ready language for it then, I knew in that instant that I was being given the ability to translate the transcendent beauty of our universe into words.

Since then, nature has been a clear, exacting teacher that shows me who I am as well as who I might become if I stay open to its wisdom. To faithfully record that essential energy—with the hope of revealing a path of truth and healing and compassion—has always seemed to me to be at the heart of being a poet.

If even one of these poems touches you and brings you to a higher place of understanding or contemplation, I will leave this place knowing that my mission here has been accomplished.

Thank you for reading them.

—Karen Mireau
February 1, 2025

TWO
THOUSAND
RAINS

something else sings

The ground goes gold and dangerous green
somewhere on the mountain the leaves brighten and flicker
here in backcountry there is no resistance to the dance
the coming of rain is a serious thing

Each hour we listen for the sound upon the stones
we hold open our eyes like children making real our imagining
but for now there is only the rasp of sparrows
combing the earth for crumbs, an eerie whisper high in the leaves

Elsewhere a tin roof chimes with northern rain
each drop a fast memory, a first tense kiss
the act of waiting is a poem spoken over and over
until it moves within us effortlessly

We fall into dreams that have no familiarity
these are not the visions we have sought these many days
but new clay turned on the wheel of the wind
so, too, the sudden storm comes to define us —

an archetypal palette of water and flame

1

And when, late, the sky gives up its whorled music
we wake to find our longing has again slipped away
swallowed by the earth's invisible bloodline
the emptied clouds' dopplered refrain

where something else
yes, something very different
now sings

blue fingers

It is the small things that set us apart
and lead us, finally, back to ourselves

That one day in early spring
it was the angulation of the rain
sweeping the dark drumlins
the crosshatching of the woods
like that of the countryside
you had been born in
that made your heart quicken
once again

You pulled the old Ford over
entranced by the choreography
of the withered grasses, the still lifeless trees
all of this so like the time
you watched, as a child
your dreaming enacted
in the progression
of a northeastern thunderstorm

Many strange configurations
followed

You had no choice
but to live as a poet
and walk with your ears locked
to every invisible chord

Years later, you realized
how far you had wandered
it was then that you desired
to rejoin the commonplace

Life became sane

You couldn't stand it
you went back to the rain's feeling language
its mysterious conjugations
you became pregnant with words
aborted, became pregnant again

you found you could kill
for the choice of poetry

It was very difficult
but it was a different sort of pain
again, it was like the sky
breaking open over Kansas

hyacinths & biscuits

Poetry is the synthesis
of hyacinths and biscuits.
— Carl Sandburg

This is the world's basic flour :
furrows of dark, damp earth
cupping a bank of wild hyacinths
iridescent with dawnlight and dew
keeping them firmly tethered to earth

To which we add the salt and the sweet :
a childhood face, burning with tears
the remembrance of our mother's cool hand
soothing our forehead
her soft voice saying, "There, now."

For moisture :
the pure milk of the last snow
turning back into rain on the roof
saying everything is emptiness
everything, too, is bliss

To make it rise :
a spring wind suffused with sparrows
and the old leaves of winter
scouring the ground
with their rascally laughter

To bind it :
a stand of sycamores, gospel grey
bowing and witnessing over the creek
suddenly you know, irrevocably
why it is they sing

And for heat :
there is the hopeful, heavenly bell that is the sun
rising to meet the hyacinth sky
igniting the tips of the flowers
and the now-violet fields beyond

This world : this bread : this common life
so perfectly filled at every moment
with both the ordinary and the sublime

**nights of small rains
grazing the meadows**

In the thick height
above the battered grass
summer was a hot wind
beating the oats love-low

Upladder
what the wind or we
could not gather
and always further than the hand

Firm as her breast at fourteen
like the speckled October air
the ground smelling of honey
cold fruit and stones

The pears break off like thunder
a full-grown vision
alight in a tree —
reach

Your timing is all

gathering violets

This is how falling in love
with the world again begins—
a series of small explosions
as the violets appear
from under the receding snow
filling the air with succulent sweetness

Their amaranthine hearts
shuddering on the slightest breeze
in time to the pale pulsing of the veins
beneath our skin
waking to the extant sexual call
the scent of newly-thawed earth

As the rains draw near
we must make our hands
slower than time
to touch as when we were children
the velvet petals of grass
so ethereal, so sanguine

Go, then, feel this —
this longing, this green torrent
of love and of grief
it is, after all a kind of magic
water and air and earth
becoming the very breath of spring

two thousand rains

I was born in the time of rain
and if the gods and goddesses are good
I will die in in the time of rain
this I know to be true —
that rain will always be
my beacon, my baptism, my shroud
my Krishna, my Buddha
my long-abandoned Christ

The town I lived in as a child
was grey as a grave, as endless as the open sea
each morning banks of clouds rolled in to stay
stone colored, unwavering
though I did not understand it then
this altered everything — every step
every path traversed
the way I saw and listened to the earth

The tattered gauze of clouds
hung over the hills, a sepulchral psalm
a continual, contextual prison
it was because of the ancient glaciers, they said
that had scoured and razed the land
a simple matter of physics
leaving behind the Great Lakes
the drumlins rising parallel to one another

Best to blame something, anything
though no one really gave it much thought
as a child, it was just the way things were
rain stitching day to night, night to day
and in between a cheerless silence
broken only by the bright messengers
of forsythia, lilac, chickadee
the great green explosion of spring

Secretly, we were the unforgiven, forever at fault
our confusion, our longing, our twisted dreams
were, like the rain, unceasing
you had to travel deep within to find even a little light
it made us strong, though not immune
to thoughts of ending things — we understood
for some of us it was the only way back
to salvation, nirvana

A taciturn child, I came to love
the grey envelopes of unspoken time
the darkness that bruised the sky
the clouds that churned like sour milk
the raging of late summer storms
some days slow, some days accelerating
beyond any imaginable sense
and the emptiness after, waiting to be filled

The whirlwinds, kicking up dust
scattering the kaleidoscope of leaves
the gently slanted showers of early spring
dampening the spongy earth like dough
the halo of after-sun : a waterfall of light
poured from some enormous jar
turning the underwoods to briny green
the ploughed fields black as veins of coal

Rain falling from the flowers mouths
causing the ground to swell and speak in return
rain changing its garments : from undyed wool
to sleek cloaks of silk and silver
the chiming of a tin roof
the spin of whirligig, weathervane
becoming whirlpool, wave,
fin, wing, a wonderful apostrophe

Rain, purifying the silence
with the sound of far-off fairy bells
the slow throaty rumble of thunder calling after
prismatic mirror of puddle and sky
traveling a trajectory
between heaven and earth
back to some secret center
where poetry and chemistry merge

If we're very lucky in this life
we see it, we feel it, we desire all of it
forgiveness and joy, birth and death
expectation, despair
each rain an echo of a grief
too fresh, too lonely to give name
each rain another chance to take a turn
around the slippery, bejeweled room

And now, when I look up at the sky
to wonder, as I often still do
I see my child self sitting by the window
watching the rain come down and down
I was born in the time of rain
and if all is good I will return the same way
rain : my baptism, my shroud, my sepulcher
the song I always listen for, and dance to

I have always known it to be true

.

while braiding onions

We know the weathervane's
intimate dark iron
we know the wind gathers
blue and unspeaking on the hill

The birds in their territories
one rings above the others, also

Having thrust your hands in
to dust, earth, matter
the rain comes
sweet as a clove

what my life has been

A joysong
a surprising sorrow
tumultuous
a river deep
a strange wood
without end, a path
through magical hollows
that comes
to the edge of a cliff

Where I stand
over and over
about to jump
and then I do jump
(or not, either way)
suddenly I am on the other side
breathing fast
amazed at the breadth
of the chasm
behind me

signs of life

After the spring turning
the ploughed furrows fill with rain
a sea of earthen waves
undulating to the horizon

The waters slowly sink
soaking into the groundswell
the blackbirds, those pirates, arrive
surveying the shores for treasure

And there you stand —
a stranger to this new land
survivor of yet another storm
yourself, yet not yourself

suddenly, irrevocably changed
walking the still-wet fields

there is no thunder in winter

In early spring
the young farmhand
on his sky-blue Spitfire Schwinn
races for the barn
in front of the lightning

I admire his enterprise
the speed he is able to gather
up and down these rough hills
his shy hellos, his loss for words

The rain follows him
a wet shadow
slicing the last ice on the creek
into grey, swanlike syllables

Afterwards
the willow trees fill with light
and Henry, the farmhand, says
quite softly
"I'd never thought of it before
but there is no thunder here in winter, is there?"

which end of the rainbow's wet eye

Who will say what it is
that waits for us?
who will be the first to say
where the end
will meet the miracle in the wheel

We loved each other
and that was enough
enough we say
to make an ending real
enough to say we loved
without hope of an end
so that here
the waiting is over

a song from unknown sources

This is really the song
of an invisible bird
translated for your own enjoyment

The song goes like this:

life is, life is
it is, is, is
just what it is

Then the rain —
that blinding-knife-edged-Bluegrass kind of rain
comes thundering down

black marks

The way rain blown by the spring storm
slashes across the red oak planks
of the tobacco barn, branding
the thirsty wood with dark exclamations
seems an unmerciful accounting—
so many things were unexpected
so many things took a turn for the worse

There was a message in every shadow
every lie, every disturbing conundrum
even so, the clues completely eluded me
(though quite possibly I wished that to be so)
then, just when all seemed hopeless
that too much was stacked against me,
the end game impossibly lost

this bitter, particular truth—
hidden for so long
so necessary for my survival
emerges from the wet grain

storm drains

In late summer came thunderstorms
and sudden deluges
that surprised even the old ones

The four of us children
found this fascinating too —
the flotsam and jetsam of our neighbors
swirling in ragged regattas
down hilly streets
where the ancient cobblestones
had worn through

To pool at the storm drains
that lay near our house
at the bottom of Redfield Place
we thought this a marvel —
now there were rivers and lakes
to splash across on our bikes
deep enough to overflow our rubber boots

Seasoned adventurers
we hunted drowned earthworms
grown long and pale as spaghetti
realizing later, only later
we were alone on the street
unkempt, motherless
the only children allowed out

the clouds getting ready once again
to break the news

spring spell

Conjure this
if you will

The quietude of the snowbells
those unassuming nuns in their neat white habits
watching over the rain-kissed crocuses —
those oh-so-precocious, crayon-colored preschoolers

Then, to follow, the staid hyacinths
resolutely standing guard
emerging as unexpected green rockets
through the newly-fallen snow

Oh, I know
you've seen this all before

The black tulips back-bending
into a row of upside-down exclamations
the oakleaf hydrangea evolving
into one of its many alien permutations

The sweet fanfare of the daffodils
renouncing the tragedy of all our suffering
and the starlings, calling and answering
"for what? for what? all for what?"

But you and I know the answer –
it is for all those who are lost, all those yet to be found

And those of us who sit in silent awe
of the perfect cataclysm
of this unraveled spring

aujourd'hui

`

for the blackbirds
at Satori Farm, Lexington, Kentucky

Hope, have hope

This, the redwing blackbirds
constantly remind me—
with or without us
the ghost ocean of dawn will return

Thickening the hollows
erasing the hills' blue outline
rendering the charcoal edges of the fields
into a far more ethereal world

Hope, have hope

This is something
I might never have taken to heart
or ever have imagined but for
the blackbirds' faithful pronouncements

One of thousands of reasons you and I
are tethered to this particular patch of earth—
here, where in each and every lifting darkness
the stuff of new dreams is being birthed

waterdance

The flowers stagger, go numb with sun
we count the days of rain on one hand
a rosary to the threat of water rationing
and those of us who still know how
begin a waterdance in our hearts

Come rain, come thunder
come lightning-filled clouds
come cool us, heal us
give us back our green ground

Come touch our face
with your church light of tears
come glisten in the cathedral pines
come rain, come grey dreams

Come mellifluous nights
come silvered air and whole harmonic roofs
come rain like holy water
rain like great mother's milk

It may be sad
but to divine requires a touch
we have not known in many, many years
yet we live in common times with common thoughts
these, too, can be put to use

So I say sing and dance the dance
as long as you can
do not be afraid to laugh out loud
when clouds begin to mass
in tandem to our funny prayers

And the unfamiliar sound
begins to pelter
through the darkening trees
where the sparrows now fold
their quiet wings

going to atlantis

I was eight and had escaped
as I so often did then
to swim alone
away from the too-watchful gaze
of the adults

(it is impossible
and quite impractical
as you know
to practice being a mermaid
in front of an audience)

That day the river current
caught and pulled me
swift and unrelenting

down
down
down

I flailed my arms, breathed water
the green gloam turning bright with fish eyes
a thousand pretty iridescent prisms
pulsing to the thunderous heartbeat
of the great St. Lawrence

Suddenly it all snapped shut
and there I was — free
deliciously in love with death
without any want or desire
sinking peacefully through the cold, quiet dark

Blank as black ice or midnight rain
alone as only pure emptiness can be
but for the Being who came and lifted me up
laying me gently on shore
almost half a mile down river

Saying:
"The story is not yet done
there is more, much more . . ."
and with the warning
not to tell, not to tell
faded from my vision

And I slept then so peacefully
in the noonday sun
my seaweed hair, my sleek fin
my memory of that day
slowly retreating

how I became a bird

Day after day
I climbed the twisted old oak
and listened to the birds' refrains

learning by heart
their leafy languages, their holy conjugations
their pitch-perfect, twin-throated melodies

I longed to kiss the very tops of the trees
to be one with the wind, the pure azurine of air
to morph from girl to my true bird spirit

so I hid in the branches
until the last screen door slammed
and all the children's voices were long gone

Hid there, so quietly
that even my mother's frantic cries
could not route me out

only then did I venture forth
never one moment of hesitation —
I was off!

Flying over fields and streams
above the rooftops of my little town
above the nimbus clouds withholding rain

No one ever saw or heard
my bird heart quicken, my twin throats
burst exquisitely into song

Or witnessed my bird feet
touch down, so tenderly
no matter

Between you and I
it was yet another
perfect landing

untold story

It began in the wood
spackled with rain and spring green
when I was three
the smallest birds
just lifting their wings
and the man on the roof
seeming so far away
hammering, hammering
while they took off my clothes
and the world then
held the sharp taste of fear
and later a stuffed, unforgiving
silence

It followed me
like a steel shadow
an untouchable part
that no sun could warm
no heaven-sent rain rinse clean
and it was that sorrow
that pulled forth my best

Drove me to rise above
the sound of hammering
that faded but never stopped
and I saw, but only much later
that to transform this
into something more than grief

was everything, just everything

there comes a time

When we long
for a secret house
made of earth or leaves
a place to shelter from the rains
our sweet miseries bring

And we start the journey
casting everything aside
not knowing, once more
who we are
or who we were

or where we'll go
from here

the opening

Hearing my footfall
on the path
the ducks on the pond
line up like guilty children

I stop
and each of us freezes
standing sentinel, senses wide
waiting for the other to take a step

I bow in reverence
and they tighten like flowers
before a rain
scattering strategically in pairs

leaving me dead center
in the middle of the farm
speechless in the hole created
by entering their sacred space

In the parity of that new silence
I stand humbled
grateful for their awareness

and to have experienced
that one moment
of their earthly, unbound grace

rainy day dress

The only dress I owned then
was brown, faded as fill dirt
covered with tiny white flowers

Cap sleeves, ivory trim
boom-boom-boom
three plastic buttons down the front

Peterpan collar
edged in Woolworth's lace
hem just grazing my scabbed-up knees

Skirt a cocoa-colored umbrella
just meant to twirl and twirl
and swirl about in

One sash end about to tear loose
but fine as fine could ever be
for dancing in the rain

See:
here I am in the photo
five years old

Bangs cut way too short
my sepia eyes a vacant lot
waiting for a reason, any reason at all

To escape my mother's gaze
and run out under
the nonjudgmental sky

the beautiful rain of the future

It is raining quietly in the dark
and when the light lifts
all is a glimmer-glow, a silken mist
in the black entangled branches
of the winter trees
a fancy cursive etching the sky

Spelling out a language
only a broken heart
can ever truly understand
and there is a light
flickering in the distance
like a new self waking

One just now seeing
the many possible colors
of the wild sky, the wetted fields

the betrayal

When it was learned
abruptly — that our entire life
as husband and wife was fiction
that every word you spoke
every kiss you metered out
everything you did was a sham

The children, fortunately
were mostly grown and gone
and once the sad inventory of our life
all the objects we thought were precious
were sorted, discarded, or given away —
before that final *au revoir*

What would remain?
but a few fading photos
to remind us of the orchards we'd planted
the now maturing fruits falling
in the receding dusk
with no one left to harvest them

It all came down to this —
a dream manifested
through sheer toil and persistence
but a life, it must also be said
often filled with simple joys
and, sometimes, perfect silences

Therein lies the sadness —
for each of us awaits down the road
for whatever time may be left us
a grieving that seems an endless rain of tears
for what our life might have been
had it been real

and the relentless memory
of that first, ill-fated kiss

spring again

There was rain
and more rain
and spring
or something like it

You felt as if
you'd been shoved
face down into a ditch
a thick, Carhartt boot
planted squarely on your neck
your mouth stuffed silent
with grief and wet grit —
so horrible, yet in some ways
tasting so sweet

And the flowers — *my oh my*
they all looked so different then
there were no more answers
no more questions
nothing more
that could possibly hurt you

yes, yes
it was pretty much
all up from there

my lilac tree

All of spring I waited
for the magic to reappear
never knowing just when
its blossoms would choose to unfurl
painting the origami dawn
with their laughing summersong

Do you still know how to talk to a tree?
my lilac heard my childhood prayers
and counted every brittle tear for me

Oh, to put a fresh spray of lilac
against my cheek
could carry me far, far away
in each small flowerlet
a fairy mirror glistened
and a secret story murmured
like the purple heart of the sea!

When the strong moon woke me
in my second-story room
I would come to the cool windowsill
and lay down my head
to pretend I was sleeping
in the smooth arms of my lilac

Rocking me sweetly
in the long and restless midnight breeze
filling my dreams
with their hopeful, leafy lullaby

A quiet one
no one ever guessed what it meant to me
to touch the tips
of its starry blossoms after a rain
to hear the invisible chiming
crystalline and amethyst

I knew then that I might make
such music as only my lilac made

and that alone
has granted me a strong heart—
the thought of a single, remembered tree
having more power to heal
than all the love medicines
on this old earth

heartfire

everything comes
everything goes

one day the ground is covered
in brown, cold heaps of earth and tattered grass
the other, sifted with autumn gold

from behind the clouds
the sun arrives
the grief that has kept us prisoner
these many days
slowly departs in as many ways as leaves
or rain would fall

everything comes
everything goes

your memory becomes a heartfire
that ignites and returns to life
whenever we choose to call it forth
oh, if only everything else on this cold earth
were that simple

the necessity of rain

I would like to live once again
where there is rain
a place you could feel
the wild stirrings a long way off

rain like a common song in the wood
rain like a code upon the windowsill

At first I would listen carefully
to the before and the after
only then would I begin to consider
the sound of the rain itself

rain like a wheel
rain like the poems inside every child's head

Bending to the arch of the wind
to the shape of the house, the fields
magnifying the ceremonious trees
waiting greyly and infinitely beyond

each rain beginning differently
and differently coming to an end

One night without even thinking
I would run from my bed out into the rain
no matter if it were cold
the rain would be calling me as it once did

rain smelling of earth and wood and ice
the wheat and marrow of another land

Dark rain in my dark hair
sweetly green in my mouth
naked, silken lavender upon my eyes
the cool glass at every pulse

rain like a second skin
rain like the memory of you

Somewhere a rain has just ended
and far off, a new one begun
the singing and bowing of the trees not far behind
and then the still, unfurling moment

rain like a coda
rain like the electric hush after making love

I believe that to be a record of this — to open wide
and welcome each day with a whole heart
and then to close, like rain, to a more intelligent quiet

could be no more honest work
for any poet

acknowledgments

In the Land of the Wahoo Trees
Azalea Art Press, 2024:
a song from unknown sources
aujourd'hui
black marks
there comes a time
what my life has been

Redfield Place
Azalea Art Press, 2022:
a song from unknown sources
going to atlantis
how i became a bird
hyacinths and biscuits
my lilac tree
rainy day dress
spring spell
storm drains

Tell Me Again |
That the Dead Do Dream | The Mendon Poems
Azalea Art Press, 2023:
blue fingers
signs of life
there is no thunder in winter

1982 Chester H. Jones Competition
nights of small rains
grazing the meadows

Karen Mireau, 2023
photo by Shoey Sindel

Karen Mireau began her professional journey as a full-time poet. She soon discovered that this sensibility lent itself perfectly to the medium of film. In Los Angeles, after working as executive assistant to NBC CEO Grant Tinker and President Brandon Tartikoff, she co-founded an animation company that created **"Kissyfur"** and **"Foofur"**—two hit Saturday morning shows for **NBC,** and many concepts for toys, books, television, and film production.

She also found a distinct flair and passion for marketing. From merchandising and promoting her own TV shows she learned the principles of bringing complex concepts successfully to their target audience.

In her early thirties, Karen had the honor and wonder of birthing a beautiful, talented daughter, Marina Leigh Mendez Williams, and helping raise an extended family of marvelous and wildly creative sons and daughters, all of whom she adores dearly to this day.

During that time, she also developed *Satori*, a permaculture farm and healing center in Kentucky based on the teachings of Rudolph Steiner, where she continued her life-long commitment as a self-avowed "Agricultural Anarchist" and "Entre-manure."

Karen continued her passion for marketing and children's media, resulting in **"Troubles the Cat,"** created with her daughter, Marina, then 5 1/2 years old. "Troubles" premiered on **Cartoon Network** in 47 countries in **Jim Henson's** series **"Big Bag"** and was produced by **Children's Television Workshop**, of Sesame Street fame and is currently being developed as a half-hour series with the original producer, internationally-renowned author, animator and filmmaker **R.O. Blechman**.

Troubles led to a natural expansion of her focus to nurture other authors, illustrators and creators of children's books, television and film. In her role as a "Literary Midwife" and founder of **Koo Koo & Company**, Karen traveled throughout the U.S. and Europe presenting children's media concepts to major publishers and distributors and launching many careers.

In 2008, Karen discovered a new direction in the form of helping others express and put their stories into print, and created **Azalea Art Press**, now an imprint of **Karen Mireau Books.** To date, she has published over 100 diverse titles—including novels, poetry, picture books, middle grade and young adult fiction, and numerous memoirs.

It's been her bliss ever since—but she has never abandoned her love for the natural world. She continues to plant gardens of nurturing food, flowers, and medicinal plants wherever she lives.

Karen now calls the wine country of Sonoma, California, home. Alongside her husband, photographer Raymond Rimmer, she continues to write, garden, paint, publish, and shower her friends, family, and grandchildren with unending affection and love.

other titles of interest
by Karen Mireau

All Their Yesterdays
Novel, 2019.

The Architect of Fire
Poems, 2024.

The Conscientious Visitor
Karen Mireau
& Marla Lay
Nonfiction, 2013.

The Cottage Hotel: The History & Untold Tales of Mendon Hamlet's Legendary Tavern & Stagecoach Inn
Local History Anthology, 2023.

The Cottage Hotel Songbook
Lyrics & Music, 2023.

Cracker Jack-Jack
Karen Mireau
& Zoey Williams
Picture Book, 2021.

Ever After : An Artist's Childhood
Karen Mireau
& Cynthia Garlock Kozlowski
Memoir, 2018.

In the Land of the Wahoo Trees
Poems, 2024.

Front Porch Lessons: The Stories of Alma & George Johnson
Memoir, 2024.

Marienau : A Daughter's Reflections
Karen Mireau
& Dr. Annemarie Roeper
Memoir, 2012.

Matsu.Kaze : The Wind in the Pines
Poems, 2016.

Oh No! Emma!
Picture Book, 2018.

Redfield Place
Poems, 2021.

Sweet Land of Liberty : 50 Years Later
Karen Mireau
& John Wedda
Illustrated book on civil rights, 2015.

Sycamore Road
Poems, 2024.

Tell Me Again | That the Dead Do Dream
Poems, 2023.

To Contact the Author
please email:
KarenMireauBooks@gmail.com

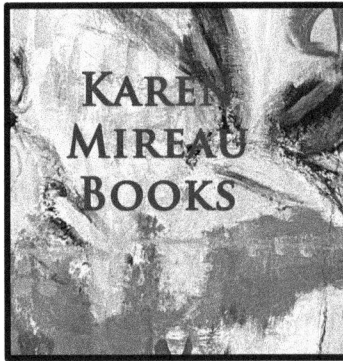

KAREN
MIREAU
BOOKS

For Direct Book Orders
www.Lulu.com

To learn more
please visit:
https://karenmireaubooks.com

www.ingramcontent.com/pod-product-compliance
Lightning Source LLC
Chambersburg PA
CBHW050356100426

42739CB00015BB/3417